W9-DDV-674
ACTION

BOOKS,

NOTRE

DAME,

INDIANA

2006

you are a little bit happier than i am

TAO LIN

———

Winner of the 2005 December Prize
First Edition
www.actionbooks.org

ACTION BOOKS
Joyelle McSweeney and Johannes Göransson, Editors
Jesper Göransson, Art Director
Kristina Sigler, Assistant Editor
John Dermot Woods, Web Design
Kwoya Fagin, 2005-2006 Editorial Intern

Action Books gratefully acknowledges the instrumental support of the University of Notre Dame.

Action Books
Department of English
University of Notre Dame
356 O'Shaughnessy Hall
Notre Dame, IN 46556-5639
Learn more about us at www.actionbooks.org.

———

some of my happiest moments in life occur on AOL instant messenger

if i get hit a little by a truck tonight i'm okay with that

i want to pour orange juice on my face

that night with the green sky

poems that look weird

spring break

things i wanted to do today

i want to start a band

i am unemployed

October

January, February, March, April, May, June, July, August, September, October, November

my favorite book of poetry right now

i saw you on the street

loneliness is just a word that means you are feeling alone and depressed and starting to think about how difficult and strangely impossible it is for you to be interested in the same people who are interested in you and how if you don't change your worldview and personality soon then you will probably always feel alone and depressed because you can't remember a time when you haven't felt alone and depressed

———

but really you can and that is when you were a small child but that small child seems like a different person, really, than who you are right now and you can't become a different person anymore because you are over twenty years old and people this age don't change unless they fall off a barn and get a long metal rod through their brain and then they change drastically and get studied by scientists and never have to get a real job again but always look very alone and far away and doomed on TV even if they and all their friends and family and an international team of doctors, neural surgeons, and psychologists— cognitive, behavioral, courtroom, and analytical—say that they aren't at all

pessimism? or robotics?

it'll get different

Friday

i am about to kill my literary agent

4:30 a.m.

thanksgiving

Appreciate Me For Everything Good I Have Done In The Past

i honestly do not know who this poem is directed at but i still somehow wrote it with conviction

I Am 'I Don't Know What I Am' And You Are Afraid Of Me And So Am I

i hate the world and i'm not immature

i am about to express myself

The Poem I Wrote In My Room After We Fought On The Internet And You Called Me A Dick And Said You Had To Go To Sleep And Said You Would Email Me Over Thanksgiving From Home But Then Said 'Forget It' After I Said About You Emailing Me Over Thanksgiving From Home That 'I Doubt It'

My Dreams Are Almost Always Nightmares In Retrospect

———

you were a martial arts master and you worked at circuit city

you published a one-page comic where someone freaks out while eating
    breakfast

an instant messenger conversation we had about how my dad was in jail

you are somewhere in florida right now

things you have emailed me

in manhattan on 29th street across the avenues then over a railing there is
    a little beach

book reviewers always praise books as 'life-affirming' because the more
    humans there are on earth the better

promise i'll vote for you

poem to end my head off

i see million dollar baby, starring clint eastwood, with my mom

you are my mom

when i think of grapefruits my heart beats faster

i am 'you' to you

Washington Mutual Is A Bank That Is Everywhere

I Will Like The Things I Dislike, Hate, Or Am Indifferent Towards

April

walking home in cold weather

my brother is vacationing on a mountain with his girlfriend
    and i found out from my dad

February

At That Leftover Crack Concert Two Years Before I Met You

some of my happiest moments in life occur on AOL instant messenger

———

i will create a new category
on my instant messenger buddy list

i will call it
'people i like who don't like me back'

and i will move your screen name into that group
and i will invite you to my house and show you

and you will say, 'if i didn't like you why did i come over'
and you will look at my face
and i will have an honest answer for your question
i will tell you that you came over to be polite

and after a while you will go home
and you won't call
and i won't either
and after a while i won't like you anymore
and after a while we'll forget each other
and after a while you will be beautiful and alone inside of your coffin
and i'll be cold and alone inside of my coffin

if i get hit a little by a truck tonight i'm okay with that

——

in a hospital the painkillers help your mood
at night you feel like a five-year-old
i don't want to be in love or win the national book award
i say, 'just let me live in a hospital for free with a lung problem'
you say, 'be careful what you wish for'
i say, 'um, why should i be careful what i wish for if i'll be happy
        if i get what i want?'
you say, 'it's hard to tell if you're being sarcastic'
i say, 'a conversation like this would never happen in a hospital'

i want to pour orange juice on my face

i want to pour a carton of orange juice onto my face and body
when i am lying on my bed, in the morning
and i want it to be sunday and i want to go back to sleep
and when i fall back asleep i want the orange juice to quickly evaporate
and take me with it

that night with the green sky

it was snowing and you were kind of beautiful
we were in the city and every time i looked up
someone was leaning out a window, staring at me

i could tell you liked me a lot or maybe even loved me
but you kept walking at this strange speed
you kept going in angles and it confused me

i think maybe you were thinking that you'd make me disappear
by walking at strange speeds and in a strange and curvy way
but how would that cause me to vanish from earth?

and that hurts
why did you want me gone?
that hurts
why?

why?
i don't know
some things can't be explained, i guess
the sky, for example, was green that night

poems that look weird

one time i wrote a poem that looked really weird
it looked like a scrabble board would
if i were playing against you and losing by three hundred
because i'd just mix up all the tiles then, and you'd be angry
but you'd laugh and that would be fun

this other time you had the paris review anthology
you were looking for a poem about boats to show me
i pointed at a poem that looked weird
i said, 'i hate it when they do that'
and you said, 'i don't; i think it's pretty'

another time i was thinking about you
i was thinking that you think weird poems are pretty
and i think you are pretty
and i was thinking there was something there, in that thought
some sort of connection that was completely free of bullshit, finally

spring break

___

it's the sunniest day ever and i'm going around thinking about my story
    collection
my eight stories about twenty-five to thirty or fifty depressed people

thinking about how none of those made-up people feel exactly like i do
they are all happier and not like me, not like i am right now
and what will i do about this, i'm thinking, how can i live with this

and i wait around for my writing professor
who will help me publish this book, who will tell me i'm self-indulgent
who i will agree with and then feel sort of hollow and good
but who doesn't show up

so i call you
the only girl in the world that i like
and you cancel on me, and you ask me

―――――

if i want you to call me over spring break
from your home
and i say if you want to

and you say you will then
and of course, maybe, you won't

and i go to the strand, buy three of the most depressing books i can find
which i know i'll never finish because they won't be depressing enough

and so i buy a six-dollar fruit tart and eat it walking around
and it feels like i'm walking on water
and i am amazed that i am not below and inside the concrete, drowning

on the train i sit and shut my eyes
i am in the middle of some stupid world and where my brain is is
instead a huge, wet heart

and where my organs are are instead hearts
and my bones are all hearts too
and no heart anywhere in the world is beating but just wet and
    humming and enormous
and i walk home

it is three p.m. and bright outside
and i know that my day is over

i lie on my bed and i wait for your phone call
the only person in the world that i like
my favorite person
not god but just a person

and i know you can't save me, you didn't create the universe in seven days
you're just another person who isn't in love with me
but maybe you can do something, still, i guess, and i want to murder you
and myself

———

and i get up and shut my door and shut the blinds and turn off every light
turn off the fan, everything

pull the covers over my face, pretend it's night
and try to view my life as ironic and humorous
try to view it in a wry and detached way

but i can't, and instead i try my hardest to cry
but that doesn't happen either, so i just lie very still
and listen for your phone call, because now i'm thinking that maybe

you canceled on me by accident
maybe you are accidentally really in love with me
maybe the devil intervened and said you'd die
if you didn't cancel, we'd both die if you didn't cancel
or something

and i am lying very still and thinking all this and time keeps going
and i know that i must fall asleep for twenty hours
can't wake up around nine p.m. rested and hungry and thinking of you
must sleep straight into tomorrow

and this is what i'm thinking
i'm thinking, please, just let me go to sleep
thinking, please, and i am listening
very closely for your phone call
and i am going a little insane
and after a long time, finally, i am insane, i am crying a little
the tiniest of cries, something miniscule and not even real
just some water behind the eyes, some salt
in the brain
not crying actually, but something else
something strange and new
a small piece of my heart, letting go
into the blood
about a hundred thousand pieces of my heart, into the blood
the whole thing, going places

things i wanted to do today

―――――

i wanted to join a water polo club
i wanted to buy a white t-shirt
i wanted to walk around for one hour staring amiably at people's faces
    as they passed by on the streets and sidewalks
i wanted to say hi to strangers and smile at them until they smiled back
i wanted to let my appetite go and go and then when i felt hollow and good i
    wanted to buy a corn muffin and a coffee and a soup and sit in the park
    on a bench and take my time eating and feeling the sun on my arms
i wanted to email or call every friend i ever had
i wanted to have initiative and make plans for as many fridays, saturdays,
    and sundays as possible for the rest of my life
i wanted to buy a small vacuum cleaner and a small fold-up desk
    and i wanted to put the vacuum cleaner on the desk and then carry
    the desk on my head down the street toward my apartment
i wanted to see a friend sitting on a stoop to my right
i wanted to stand there listening to what they've been up to and then when
    they asked if i was uncomfortable standing there with the desk and
    vacuum cleaner on my head i wanted to say something to indicate that
    i was but that it was worth it to listen to them tell me about what has
    been going on in their life
i wanted to offer to vacuum their house
i wanted the friend to be someone i knew in fourth grade who said she
    liked me
i wanted to go in there and vacuum her house and then when she offered
    me lemonade i wanted to compliment her hair and maybe her teeth
i wanted to keep complimenting her until she was giggling and sitting
    at one end of her large couch and touching her hair and glancing at me
i wanted to put the desk in the middle of her living room and put the

    vacuum cleaner on top of the desk and then stand arms akimbo
        and say, 'well there then'
i wanted to sit on the other end of her large couch and ask her from across
        the length of the room what she was doing on friday
i wanted the TV to be off but the fan to be wooden and on and making
        a faraway and sandy noise like a beach shore
i wanted her to crawl toward me over her couch
i wanted to stand up while she was crawling toward me and vacuum
        her couch
i wanted to vacuum her hair
i wanted to say, 'can i try something on you?'
i wanted us to take turns doing new and interesting things with the
        vacuum cleaner
i wanted us at one point to be standing on the desk together trying to gain
        control of the vacuum cleaner from the other person
i wanted her to go in the kitchen and come back in the living room with a
        steak knife and i wanted her to chase me with it
i wanted to leave her house when the sun was big and red and the sky was
        orange and whipped like a peach smoothie
i wanted on the way home to see a three-year-old boy with black hair and
        blue eyes playing with a small white dog
i wanted to shower with hot water and then cold water and then walk
        around naked
i wanted to do one hundred jumping jacks to build my stamina
i wanted to cut up a papaya and eat it
i wanted to package some of my books and send one to my mom, one to
        my brother, one to a friend
i wanted to do nice things for everyone i ever knew
i wanted to lie on my bed and put my ear on the pillow
i wanted a mysterious noise outside to wake me up
i wanted the window to be open and a light breeze coming in and i wanted
        it to be dark outside and cool in the room when the mysterious noise
        woke me up
i wanted to feel sleepy and happy and comfortable
i wanted to fall back asleep wondering what the mysterious noise was that
        woke me up

i want to start a band

———

i want everyone in the band to be friends
but i also want to have complete creative control
and for everyone to be a little bit afraid of me

during practice i want to sing into my microphone
that i want to speak to my bassist in private
when privacy happens i want to tell my bassist to do more triplets
and chords

———

i want him to get a little bit angry
but then use that anger to play some really good triplets and chords

i want my guitarist to be my jealous girlfriend
and i want my drummer to have a secret crush on me
and to communicate her attraction to me through her drum-playing

one day at practice i will make a new song with only drums and singing
my guitarist girlfriend will be so jealous that she'll pretend to leave me
when i don't beg her to come back she'll just quietly come back on her own
and pretend like nothing happened

but immediately i'll write a song called 'bad and immature'
and i'll write it so my girlfriend will have to double the vocals the entire song
    for harmony
and the lyrics will consist of this one line repeated forty times
'i pretended to leave you because i am a bad and immature person'

and during shows i'll pretend my microphone broke whenever we do
    that song
so that my jealous girlfriend will have to sing it by herself to fulfill her
    vocal harmony responsibilities
and she will sound really bad and off-key because i will have written her
    harmony in tritones and half-steps

also, at one point, i want to give my bassist rules
like, i'll say to him, 'you're only allowed to play a note when the bass drum
    plays a note and it has to be exactly when the bass drum plays a note
    and it has to still sound good'
every time he screws up i'll make him do fifty push-ups
and while he's doing push-ups i'll force the rest of the band to sing the
    clown song
that song they play when someone is juggling and riding a unicycle
and if that doesn't satisfy me
then i'll stand on my bassist's back while he's doing push-ups
and paralyze him from the neck down

i am unemployed

———

i wake up at 2 p.m.
i am alert
i feel strange and alert
panic is moving through me, tentatively, like it's not sure of itself
panic is saying, 'is this right?'
my panic is saying, 'is this how to do it? slowly like this?' and i am saying,
    'yes, just keep on moving through me and never go away, that's it,' and
    i am being sarcastic, but my panic has no sense of irony and it gets a
    little confident and moves through me a little quicker now and it is
    smiling now too and moving through me with confidence and speed
and then it is nighttime and i am in bed and can't sleep
because in my head it sounds like this:

AHHHHHHHHHHHHHHHHHH
AHHHHHHHHHHHHHHHHHH
AHHHHHHHHHHHHHHHHHH
AHHHHHHHHHHHHHHHHHH

but really it doesn't even sound like that, but this:

ahhh, ahhhh, ahh, ahhhhhhhhhhhh

and that sounds really nice
and i fall calmly asleep
and the next day i am on the seventh floor at a job interview
and the interviewer is asking me a question that i will have to answer in ten
    seconds and i think it might be a three-part question and i feel kind of
    alone in the world, on the seventh floor and lonely, and even though
    i am staring at the interviewer's face and mouth i am not really paying
    attention because my hand is in my pocket and i am shocked at how
    much stuff i have in there

and it is a mystery, really, what might be in there, and i cannot resist this
    mystery and so i close my hand on some of the stuff and slowly take
    my hand out of my pocket while staring at the interviewer's face and

———

then glance and see that in my hand in my lap there is a package of
mixed nuts, a metrocard, a five-dollar bill, a piece of yarn, sunglasses,
and a scrap of paper that says 'prepare for the interview or else you are
a worthless piece of shit' on it and i feel afraid and doomed and i know
that i am on the seventh floor and a little lonely
and then the interview is over and i stand and smile and the interviewer
does not stand but smiles up at me and i laugh and she laughs and
i say, 'i hope to speak to you soon,' and she says, 'it was nice talking to
you,' and i laugh and she laughs and i think i might ask her for a walk in
the park even though she is sixty years old but so what because we can
be best friends and finally learn something about life and mortality and
death and other things you learn when you hang out with someone
forty years older than yourself but then i am in the elevator and then
i am outside

i buy bottled water
i say to myself, 'give up'
my brain says, 'yeah, just give up'
i say to my brain, 'when i run out of money i'll just curl up on the sidewalk
and eventually i'll disappear'
my brain says, 'drink your bottled water'
and i say, 'no, not yet'
because i know that secretly i want my bottled water to hire me
i want my bottled water to be the C.E.O. of a corporation and for it to
emanate an aura of hiring me; and i want the C.O.O. of that corporation
to be trained in interpreting emanations of bottled water and be
watching us and approach from a distance and tap my shoulder and
say, 'hey, i think the C.E.O. is emanating an aura of wanting to hire you
for a part-time job that pays full-time'

i look around
my brain says, 'do something'
i go into a deli and feel afraid
because i am holding bottled water and they will think i stole it even though
i waved it in the air at the deli owner right when i went in; because he
might forget that i waved it at him and shoot me in the back with a

copper bullet because he might hallucinate and think that my bottled
water is a grenade because it looks like a grenade actually

i leave the deli
on the sidewalk my bottled water says, 'hey, calm down, just drink me'
i say, 'i know'
and i fidget
i say, 'i was going to drink you anyway, even if you didn't say that, so don't
    think i'm drinking you just because you said that'
and i open my bottled water
and i say, 'i am superior to you and you can't control me'
and i quickly drink my entire bottled water before it can respond to what
    i said and the water is cold and it goes directly to my heart and my
    heart pumps it like blood to my brain and my brain squirms and my
    heart says, 'take that,' and my brain says, 'AHHHHARRRRRGHHHHHH!'
    and my brain says, 'just kidding; i just wanted to scream,' and i go home
    and lie on my bed and roll over and i am having a nightmare

but the nightmare is like a movie and the plot is both coherent and
    convoluted and i am impressed and it has a large cast of restless and
    eccentric characters and i think it might be directed by woody allen
    even though it is a psychological thriller because the dialogue is pretty
    great and someone does a somersault and stabs someone in the heart
    and cartwheels into a pit of fire and this is all essential to the plot and
    there are themes also and it is really well-written and i think i might
    want to give it the national book award and i am writing an essay on it
    and having footnotes and extrapolating those footnotes into a second
    essay that is critical of the national book award people for excluding my
    nightmare from its award just because my nightmare isn't a book and
    i am angry at the world and i am pitching both these essays to harper's
    while still writing them inside of my nightmare and watching my
    nightmare like a movie and i am writing the first line of the second essay
    and the first line that i am writing is, 'the worst award committee of its
    generation,' and then the nightmare is over and the ending does not
    disappoint at all but teaches me—not rhetorically but epiphanously—to
    not be angry at the national book award people but to channel that

anger into taking a hammer into a forest and attacking wild animals
and smashing trees and wearing an owl suit and dropping out of tall
trees like a real owl and screaming and mauling campers and smashing
deer and paralyzing them and eating them alive and i think that wait a
minute, that seems wrong, is bad advice maybe; but then it seems that
there is a prologue to my nightmare and i watch it and enjoy it and it is
horrifying and shocking and it is in pill form and i swallow it and it
changes everything and it's brilliant and i wake up smiling

i shower

put on sunglasses

and go outside

it feels like i am dreaming because every light is green

but really only the first two lights are green

the third is red

and i feel disappointed that i am not inside of a dream

and at the next red light i am still disappointed and my disappointment
says, 'i dare you to keep walking even though the light is red,' and i say,
'no,' but i was being sarcastic when i said 'no,' and so i keep walking
even though the light is red and a bus almost kills me but doesn't and
honks and keeps honking even when it is at the next block because it
thinks it'll use honking as a kind of siren and that that'll actually work
and my heart is beating very hard and people are staring at me
because they are angry that i risked my life and it's hard for them to
articulate why they must be angry about how i just risked my life but
they know they are angry and that is good enough and i am wearing
sunglasses and i stand there and my brain releases adrenaline and
i feel alive

―――――

and the light turns green and all the people who are furious at me cross the
street and turn their heads and stare disapprovingly at me except for
one person who grins at me and my brain gets confused and releases
more adrenaline and then my brain says, 'wait; let me try something,'
and releases more adrenaline, all of it, and i feel so alive and restless and
ambitious and maybe even happy and my brain says, 'yeah, just make
it be happiness,' and i say, 'okay, i will'

and i do it

i am happy

my brain says, 'don't waste this'

i say, 'i know,' and i go into a deli and stand there
and my brain says, 'this is a deli'
and i turn and leave and when i am outside i run away because i feel afraid
that the deli people must think i did something devious and financially
crippling to them because i went in there and stood there and didn't buy
anything and ran away and that can only mean one thing which is that i
robbed them deviously which is even worse than robbing them
straightforwardly because at least in a straightforward situation they
would know what was happening and would feel psychologically stable
instead of psychologically destabilized which is how i feel

and i see a bookstore across the street and the bookstore says, 'hi'

i sprint wildly across the street and into the bookstore because i am in love
with anything that says hi to me on its own volition and i look at all the
literary magazines

they all say, 'read me'
and i stare at them
and one of them says, 'i rejected all your stories'
but then it says, 'buy me'
and soon they are all saying, 'buy me'

——————

and i go to the café
and eat a cookie
and the cookie says, 'thank you'
and i go to the fiction section and i see a literary magazine on the floor
and it is saying, 'subscribe to me'
it's saying, 'don't ignore me'
it says, 'save me'
and it says, 'donate and you get a free t-shirt'
but i have sunglasses on and so i can pretend that i don't see things even
    when i am staring directly at them and so i pretend that i didn't see the
    literary magazine or hear it because when you wear sunglasses you can
    also pretend that you don't hear things and people accept that and so i
    step over the magazine and then it is nighttime and i am in bed and
    having another nightmare

but this time there is no plot or theme and i am writing an essay about how
    the book of my nightmare shouldn't even have been published and was
    only published because of connections in the publishing industry and
    because of how good-looking and charismatic and good at networking
    the author of the book of my nightmare is but i am not even writing that
    essay because i am inside of my nightmare and i created it and part of
    my nightmare is that i have no creativity and can't write and now i am
    pitching the essay that i can't write to harper's but i pitch it to the
    unabomber by accident instead of harper's because this is a nightmare
    and not funny at all but deadly serious because this nightmare has no
    sense of humor and i think it might be about death but i know it isn't
    because this nightmare has no theme or meaning and six weeks later the
    unabomber sends me a form-letter rejection of my essay proposal but i
    send it again to him because maybe one of the unabomber's interns
    rejected me and i really need to have the unabomber's approval and this
    time he responds in one week with a handwritten note praising my prose
    but he also sends me a bomb and the bomb explodes and i am dying
    and i can't remember anymore what the essay i was going to write is
    about and at the end of my nightmare my nightmare cartwheels out of
    itself and runs away into my real life

October

——

At dinner your friend took your cell phone from your bag and took a photo of me and put your cell phone in your bag. Everyone noticed and I think everyone thought about it too but no one said anything even though everyone probably felt either good or bad or serious after thinking about it.

Someone said something about using dogs to fish for sharks and I sipped your drink and I said I felt drunk.

You stared at the left side of my face. You said you were going to make me uncomfortable. Your plan was to make me feel uncomfortable and you moved your face close to mine and stared and I felt serious and melodramatic because I wanted to turn and surprise you and kiss your mouth.

The waiter brought you another drink and the waiter left and you said you didn't want another drink.

I said that I'll have it and I said to give it to me.

―――――

'I don't drink,' I said.

'Yeah you do!' you said. 'You told me you wanted to get drunk and throw things in Times Square.'

'I don't get drunk,' I said.

Your friend said she was an intern for Annie Proulx's literary agent.

I left the table and tripped and fell against a wall and recovered and bumped into a silver thing that was there. The bathroom door had no handle and I couldn't get in. I couldn't tell which was the men's room because I couldn't read the writing on either door. On my way back I felt lost and walked into low benches and strange structures that were silver. You watched me and laughed and you glanced at your friend and you glanced at my friend.

I sat down. I sat there and it was the end of something and I felt calm and then I felt afraid. We ate food. You said you Googled me and read my stories and you unfocused your eyes a little and grinned.

My friend looked at me and asked me about Benjamin Kunkel.

'His book is like chick-lit,' I said. 'It's stupid.'

'Good,' my friend said.

I said my book was rejected by twenty people. You said my book was coming out soon. I said I was lying when I told you about the three-hundred-thousand-dollar advance.

You made my friend admit that animals feel pain.

'See,' you said.

I felt compassion and the compassion tricked me and I thought we were all in one family including me and you and dogs and sharks and would all love each other this year, the next year, on holidays and birthdays, and inside of hospitals at the ends of our lives.

For a moment it felt like that but it was just a moment and I don't remember what it felt like.

Outside I patted your head and you kicked my legs.

My friend left and I walked behind you. I wanted to visit your new apartment.

You said I could tomorrow and you bought tea from the grocery store.

I put grocery things in your pockets. I said you would be arrested.

Your friend was serious and she walked around being serious. She walked somewhere and came back.

'Where did you go?' I said.

She said something about cookies and looked very serious.

I found you and I put a can of something in your front pocket and you laughed and your nose changed colors.

At the cash register I felt you looking at me.

At the entrance your friend said Annie Proulx made eighty thousand a month in royalties. I calculated in my head eighty thousand a month for twelve months. I saw some plastic shopping baskets and I went there and I stepped in them and I stepped out of them.

I felt confused and I wanted to jump over the railing and do something fun but I wasn't sure if anything would be fun or just stupid and boring. I thought that the night was over and probably the week too or maybe the rest of the year and I felt serious. And I looked at my shoes.

January, February, March, April, May, June, July, August, September, October, November

----

I grinned a lot when we met. You said I was smirking. I said I didn't know what a smirk was and we had food at a café. I was looking at you and you stood to pay and I saw that you were holding yourself in a position and maybe a little nervous.

At night we walked and the buildings were pretty and everyone who was outside was happy. And I really wanted to have something.

In February I was lying on your floor. 'Why are you so miserable,' you said, and grinned. 'I will go in front of a bus if I leave,' I said. 'I'm kicking you out of my room,' you said. 'I hate you,' I said. 'I hate you too,' you said. 'I don't hate you,' I said and patted your head, and left.

I saw you in November in a grocery store. I made fun of your skirt and you said I was a jerk. You said I was a jerk again and you left and later you called. At a café I sat down. But a door was sitting where I should be sitting so I moved my chair. And moved it closer to you, very close to you.

'Stop it,' you said. 'You're freaking me out.'

I moved closer and grinned.

'I'm serious,' you said.

'It feels like I'm interviewing you,' I said.

'Describe yourself in three words,' I said.

'Vegan,' you said.

I wasn't looking at your eyes and it was almost dusk and it was like it was the future and you were dead and everything was quiet and there was a silent destruction everywhere that was quickly happening but couldn't be seen or heard or known.

'Short,' you said very loudly, and looked to your left. 'Loud.'

my favorite book of poetry right now

─────

i want every poem to be weary with itself and afraid of the world
i want all the line breaks to be where you naturally pause
i want every last stanza to not be there
and i don't want any happy poems for variety
because that is selling out
i don't care how little money you make
because selling out is a figure of speech
and i don't think you should lie to me with any nature poems
because you know you don't think sand is beautiful
unless you're in a good mood; which you never are
and i don't want any acknowledgement page because you don't have
    any friends

i saw you on the street

——

i went away

i saw other things

———

i went away some more

it rained

it did something else

it did almost all the rest of it

it was a thing too and it wanted to happen

'i am bored,' it said

'tao,' it said

i went away from it

i got away and stood there

somewhere

i don't know

there was nothing to do

i was far away from things

but things were everywhere

and i was a thing anyway

a thousand pages of reasons said i was just a thing

every reason was good and supported by footnotes

the font was huge but on each successive page the font got smaller

––––––

'it would take a long time to refute all that,' i said

i sat down

it was raining

every five minutes the thing nearest me changed into a mistake and
    disappeared

sometimes a beach ball came from the darkness and i hit it back into the
    darkness

after a while someone turned on all the lights

i was in a bright room

everyone was there

the person who i threw cherry tomatoes at the library with from a balcony
    across the street in college was there

someone in back was saying, 'i think i would almost rather be unsuccessful
    and unhappy than successful and happy'

cake was coming

a human who looked trustworthy said that you were looking for me

and gave me a beer

i cried

something good was about to happen

i cried and the crying made me sad

loneliness is just a word that means you are feeling alone and depressed and starting to think about how difficult and strangely impossible it is for you to be interested in the same people who are interested in you and how if you don't change your worldview and personality soon then you will probably always feel alone and depressed because you can't remember a time when you haven't felt alone and depressed but really you can and that is when you were a small child but that small child seems like a different person, really, than who you are right now and you can't become a different person anymore because you are over twenty years old and people this age don't change unless they fall off a barn and get a long metal rod through their brain and then they change drastically and get studied by scientists and never have to get a real job again but always look very alone and far away

and doomed on TV even if they and all their friends and family and an international team of doctors, neural surgeons, and psychologists—cognitive, behavioral, courtroom, and analytical—say that they aren't at all

———

on the internet you say you hate people
i say i hate people a lot more than you do

we are at a restaurant
everyone is talking
i feel sad and frustrated
because that is how i feel when i am around people
i hear you say that you hate people
i say that i hate people way more than you hate people

in the train station you are talking
i move very close to you
i hug you a little while you are telling me something
you laugh and twist away and take my banana and throw it in the trash

on the train i put on sunglasses
i say i wear sunglasses all the time now
you ask why
i say so people can't see the weakness in my eyes

it is the next night and four in the morning

pessimism? or robotics?

---

i am able to sit through an extremely funny movie
without making a noise or changing my facial expression

i am incapable of laughing without trying to laugh

i am never interested in anyone
unless they first show interest in me

i try not to think of myself as a person
but a metal object, built suddenly by machines in complete darkness
something impossible to hurt with a shovel

it'll get different

at work i wonder
if i should take anti-depressant medicine

finally, i decide, no, i shouldn't

later i am feeling really depressed
do it, i say, take anti-depressant medicine

still later i feel better
anti-depressant medicine, i say, ha, ha
ha, ha, ha, ha, ha, ha, ha

an hour later i catch myself thinking extremely hard
about a bright green apple being where my heart should

you are shorter than i am
you laugh louder
you laugh more
you make the face of a hamster and ask me what i think
you build a fort in your room
and i tear it down by accident

Friday

———

I woke up at 12:30 p.m. and sat on my bed. I emailed people and ate cereal and that took three hours because I took my time. When I finished I didn't know what to do so I emailed some more people.

'All I've done today is email people and eat cereal,' I emailed someone. It was 4:30 p.m. and I showered. I put on clothes. I lay on my bed and put on sad music and my hair was wet and I felt lonely.

I got up and went to a reading at a bar and ate salad. I ordered fries and said, 'I'm starving.' My friend's friend said, 'Why did you order salad then.' I wanted to ignore her but we were looking directly at each other. Everyone else was staring at me. I said something about bread and a few of them laughed. My friend was nice to me and I liked him. I said, 'I'm going to the library,' and we said goodbye.

Outside, I thought I saw someone I knew and I felt afraid.

In my room, I lay on my bed and listened to music. 'I cannot fall in love, I cannot fall in love, I cannot fall in love,' said the music. I turned the volume down and thought about tomorrow.

i am about to kill my literary agent

---

if my literary agent doesn't call me within ten minutes saying he sold my
    book i think i might do something
whatever i do it might be against the law and the police will want to
    handcuff me
if i were a cop i would arrest myself just to see what happens
i would steal someone's fur coat from their body then smash my own hand
    with my billy club
then arrest myself for assaulting a police officer
then go home and eat pasta
but if a real police officer arrested me i would feel afraid
i think i would feel so afraid that i would disappear
and that's perfect because i can kill anyone i want if i'm a ninja with the
    magic to disappear
i can kill my literary agent's entire family
just kidding
some of you just thought, 'it's wrong to kill the wife and the children'
but really i'm kidding
even though i shouldn't be
since it's probably philosophically sound to kill people
because life is suffering and suffering is the only real evil
and if you want to have meaning then that's pretty much all you get
to make it your goal to wake up and kill people
not just select kinds of people, like hitler did, but all people, like the universe
    did in the future

4:30 a.m.

---

i am biting my fingernails in bed
i am fucked existentially
i am not an okay person
i am nervous in my bed alone in my room
i am fucked existentially
i am just a normal person
i am fucked existentially
i am fucked existentially
i am fucked existentially
i am fucked existentially
i am fucked existentially
please keep reading
i am fucked existentially
i am fucked existentially
i am fucked existentially
i am fucked existentially
i am fucked existentially
i am fucked existentially
i am fucked existentially
i am fucked existentially
i am fucked existentially
i am fucked existentially
i am fucked existentially
i am fucked existentially
i am fucked existentially
i am fucked existentially
i am fucked existentially
i am fucked existentially
i am fucked existentially
i am fucked existentially

i am fucked existentially
i am fucked existentially
i am fucked existentially
i am fucked existentially
i am fucked existentially
i am fucked existentially
i am fucked existentially
i am fucked existentially
i am fucked existentially
i am fucked existentially
i am fucked existentially
i am fucked existentially
i am fucked existentially
i am fucked existentially
i am fucked existentially
i am fucked existentially
i am fucked existentially
i am fucked existentially
i am fucked existentially
i am fucked existentially
i am fucked existentially
i am fucked existentially
i am fucked existentially
i am fucked existentially
i am fucked existentially
i am fucked existentially
i am fucked existentially
i am fucked existentially
i am fucked existentially
i am fucked existentially
i am fucked existentially
i am fucked existentially
i am fucked existentially
i am fucked existentially
i am fucked existentially
thank you for reading my poem

thanksgiving

―――

i feel most comfortable around middle-class japanese people
i know they are all thinking the same things as me

WHY ARE THE LINES SO LONG?
WHY AM I IN NEW JERSEY?

though their faces appear calm
their thoughts are exactly like i just put them

also

about how we cannot communicate in our first languages:

we don't care
we don't want to communicate at all
we just want to get our food
and eat it

and go home
and go to sleep

or else go home
and discover a secret passageway behind the refrigerator
and move the refrigerator back to where it was
and take a shower
and go to sleep

Appreciate Me For Everything Good i Have Done in The Past

———

When you die, the world changes
into a funhouse. The funhouse is far away. It collapses
at the speed of light.

I just made that up.

I live in a high-density urban area.

I am hard-working,
detail-oriented; an excellent multi-tasker.
My demeanor in social situations
can be described as 'low-level panic attack.'
I am honest, tactful, and ironic.
I enjoy screaming. I think it's funny when people scream.

I think the Nobel Prize is funny.

'I am going to email a shitload of people tonight.' I think that's funny.

I feel angry. No I don't. I am bored.
I don't understand how a number can be negative. One apple
looks like one apple. What does negative-one apple look like?

The world is stupid.

The world I exist in
is really stupid.

I can prove it

at night. In the park, at night
I can prove anything.

i honestly do not know who this poem is directed at but i still somehow wrote it with conviction

————

your philosophy of life is that drugs are cool
you are so nihilistic that you don't care about the environment
your worldview is that violence, offending people, and killing animals are
    the best
your belief system is that tonight you are going to get fucked up
you are an asshole to other people because of the human condition,
    existentialism, and your high IQ
you would rather punch someone in the face and kill them than have them
    think you might be gay
your greatest accomplishment in life is that you are not a homosexual

i Am 'i Don't Know What i Am' And You Are Afraid Of Me And So Am i

___

I am so afraid of myself that my afraidness scares you more than it scares me. I should rule your life because when I do you'll be so afraid of my afraidness that you'll smash your own face with your iPod tonight because why are you listening to music when people in Africa are being terrorized by werewolves and all over the world bears are climbing buildings and falling off and falling on baby carriages and old women? In December a rat will climb in your mouth and down your throat and that's healthier than eating steak because it's organic. I'm like Hitler only agoraphobic and committing genocide against my own face nightly by looking in the mirror and you need that because human beings deserve to die. I am a rocket scientist and I miscalculated and sent the space shuttle across the street. It drove across the street and that was it. Because fuck NASA for going to the moon when there are ghosts on Earth that need to have rocket capabilities in order for them to haunt faster and haunt my house because I am afraid of them and need them to actually haunt my house so that I can complain about that and not be called paranoid or delusional or whatever. Fuck human beings. Right now I cut my face with a molar that I extracted from my own mouth with a nail clipper and I think it's infecting so come decapitate me and I'll vomit on your face. Put my brain in a knapsack and put the knapsack in your bathtub and elect your bathroom to dictate your life because shitting and pissing are the most reliable pleasures there are in life because life is a metaphor for itself and I don't know what that means and you don't either but you pretended you did for a moment there, didn't you, because you don't think for yourself and a few months ago they got giant squid on tape and you thought that was mysterious and cool but in reality the giant squid struggled for four hours before amputating its own tentacle to escape. So fuck humankind and scientists and NASA and I hope a meteor falls on the top of your skull tonight when you are making promises on AOL instant messenger that you will never keep to people who like you and who you make promises to just to keep them around so you can feel good about yourself and fuck you because of that and I should be the president of the country in which you live because I will go on TV and give you step-by-step directions that will help you commit suicide immediately and painlessly because I am compassionate which means that I want everyone to be quiet.

i hate the world and i'm not immature

---

my favorite book isn't fight club
i don't listen to death metal or limp bizkit
i'm not fourteen years old
i don't worship satan
i don't hate god
i don't go around saying everything's meaningless
i don't act like i'm a character from a bret easton ellis novel
but i am going to die
and so is everyone's mom and dad
and my brain won't ever fit in anyone else's skull
and no one will ever invent a time machine
and if i had three wishes
i wouldn't be able to sleep
and i would feel like shit all the time
finally i'd wish i didn't have three wishes
then i'd feel cheated and want those wishes again
and i'd wish for a million wishes
but the genie would be like, 'you can't do that; it's against the rules'
and i'd be like, 'what, do you work at burger king or something;
      think for yourself'
and i'd punch the genie in the face
and my fist would go through his face
and the genie would laugh at me
and later on, a year later, i'd make eye contact with the genie, in a park
and i'd avert my eyes wildly

i am about to express myself
___

i want to check my email
i want to see a movie
i want to kill people
feels like i need to kill someone
i want to kill you
i hate everything

———

why do i hate so much
everything is a lot of things
talk to me now
please talk to me
i want you to talk to me
i want you to talk to me about how i want to kill my email
i wish i loved everything
i just want to express myself
i am expressing myself right now
good
thank you
i'd like to see a movie and kill someone
i need to check my email then kill myself
i know that good news will arrive only by email
i'd like to see a movie with you then go home and check my email
can we kill someone in a supermarket
it's better in a supermarket because of contrast
the world has no contrast
i need to resurrect someone
there will be shockingly good news about my life inside of my email
killing people is immature
i am twenty-two years old
i think something happened to me
i think email changed me
i think you and email teamed up in the night and changed me in the
     daytime when i wasn't looking
i think i'd like to make out with you in a movie theatre
i admit that you are better than email
and after the movie you can stab me in the neck
if anyone else stabbed me in the neck i would feel frustrated
if you stabbed me in the neck with a fork i think i would feel pretty confident
     existentially
i would fall towards you and you would hold me
i do not want to end this poem with that line
i want to end it with some other line
i want to end my life

―――――

i don't want to end my life anymore
i changed
people change
poodles also change
i am expressing myself pretty good right now
i want to express existential despair with a hammer
i want to express the meaninglessness of life with a knife and a ski mask
i think i can do it
do you think i can do it
can we have a conversation about that
what if i stabbed you in the arm with this poem
i think this poem is serrated
i think the top of this poem is like a handle
i think i wish everything was something else
i think that is my problem
i think my problems live in a house on a mountain in north carolina
i think they are planning to come gouge me and kill me
i have anxiety
i have personal belongings that give my anxiety and make me feel serious
i want my face to be a smooth stone in a cold stream
i want an earthquake to shake me
i do not want to die today or any day
i want something cataclysmic to happen in a faraway place
i want to witness a major event
i want to be indicted for a terrible crime that has occurred on pluto
i want to plead guilty but be acquitted on all charges because of honesty
i am bored
i am expressing myself
i am sitting inside your house
i lied
i just lied
i am sitting inside my parent's house
i just told the truth
one time i told you that i felt like i was suffocating
i said i needed coffee and couldn't breathe
you were on the street going in the other direction and i followed you

The Poem i Wrote in My Room
After We Fought On The
internet And You Called Me A
Dick And Said You Had To Go To
Sleep And Said You Would
Email Me Over Thanksgiving
From Home But Then Said
'Forget it' After i Said About

You Emailing Me Over Thanksgiving From Home That 'i Doubt it'

A metal rod a lot longer than my head
can fit easily in my head.
I don't want to think about it. I want to rearrange furniture
using telekinesis. I will make my bed
go through a wall. My bed will bump people
at Whole Foods, in the cereal aisle. 'Sorry,' my bed will say, and feel
    ashamed.
And cereal will feel ashamed. But what would happen
if you were a non-sentient being. And I was god.
I think an unrelated third party would suffer.
I think I would like to break all the secret records.
The one for most consecutive days of quality over quantity.
Or just into your email
account. Because I like you very much, it is sad

that if I were you
you would be someone else. A disaster I think just happened
in the room that I am currently in. But I didn't see. And it was sleeping
when it happened. And it didn't happen. Carp had a secret.
It involved a beautiful muffin, a reoccurring dream,
and a kind of yearning that causes muffin shops to go non-profit.
Carp don't have that anymore. Last week I saw TV snow when no TV was
    in the room.
I was staring at my pillow. My head was on it. When I was four
I stabbed live fish
in their faces. Every fish I stabbed
went to secret heaven. Secret heaven is the one where
the other heaven is called secret heaven. At night in secret heaven no one
    knows what to do.
Sometimes in secret heaven everyone is afraid of secret heaven.
My bed is thinking about secret heaven.

My Dreams Are Almost Always Nightmares in Retrospect

———

You were in my dream.
You kissed my mouth. I made a face. At a water park
we made out. People were bored.
Wading pool with thousands of people

———

lying on rafts, unafraid of sharks. Chris Ringer was there.
Chris Ringer is a real person, with feelings. Chris Ringer is his real name.
Chris Ringer was at the water park. You liked Chris Ringer
more than you liked me. Chris Ringer
has taken over this poem. Chris Ringer is standing there, or something,
in my place. His name is complete,
has titanium armor
on the sides and tops. The bottom and ends have spikes
with eyes. It is a complete success
in terms of hurting me. You are in love
with him. And there he is. Shiny,
witty. Other things.

Chris Ringer. Chris Ringer. Chris Ringer. Chris Ringer. Chris Ringer. Chris Ringer.

Chris Ringer. Chris Ringer. Chris Ringer. Chris Ringer. Chris Ringer. Chris Ringer.

Chris Ringer. Chris Ringer. Chris Ringer. Chris Ringer. Chris Ringer. Chris Ringer.

Chris Ringer. Chris Ringer. Chris Ringer. Chris Ringer. Chris Ringer. Chris Ringer.

Chris Ringer. Chris Ringer. Chris Ringer. Chris Ringer. Chris Ringer. Chris Ringer.

Chris Ringer. Chris Ringer. Chris Ringer. Chris Ringer. Chris Ringer. Chris Ringer.

Chris Ringer. Chris Ringer. Chris Ringer. Chris Ringer. Chris Ringer. Chris Ringer.

Chris Ringer. Chris Ringer. Chris Ringer. Chris Ringer. Chris Ringer. Chris Ringer.

Chris Ringer. Chris Ringer. Chris Ringer. Chris Ringer. Chris Ringer. Chris Ringer.

Chris Ringer. Chris Ringer. Chris Ringer. Chris Ringer. Chris Ringer. Chris Ringer.

Chris Ringer. Chris Ringer. Chris Ringer. Chris Ringer. Chris Ringer. Chris Ringer.

They paid to get in.

you were a martial arts master and you worked at circuit city

―――――

you were in my art class in high school
we saw a movie together
you asked me why i didn't have more friends
you asked it in a nice way; like based on what you knew about my
    personality, appearance, and demeanor you just thought that i should
    probably have some more friends
and i said something about circuit city
and you said something about circuit city
and i said something else about circuit city
and you said something about your martial arts teacher being an asshole
and i said something about how i jump-kicked my brother one time and
    missed and made a hole in the wall

you published a one-page comic where someone freaks out while eating breakfast

———

i had a lorrie moore novel and you said i had it to steal from her
you stepped on my foot and looked at yourself stepping on my foot
you introduced me to your boyfriend in st. mark's bookstore
you wore an outfit that made you look like you hated capitalism and would
    throw a grenade at mcdonald's and write communist poetry in your
    jail cell
you ran away after class
i wanted to make a joke about how you probably stole something
i ran after you
i asked you if you had a plane to catch
you asked me if i was flying back to florida

an instant messenger conversation we had about how my dad was in jail

i said my plans for tomorrow were to wake up at six p.m. and buy my dad
    a present
you asked what i was getting my dad, an underground tunnel?
i said a get-out-of-jail-free card from a monopoly set
you said for christmas you were going to cry a little, then go to sleep
i said my eyes just became watery because of emotion and i dabbed my
    face with kleenex and then sighed contentedly
you said nice use of conjunctives
i asked if anyone we knew was successful
you said you file shit at an office
i said you should file folders with a fishing pole and grin at your boss
you told me to come over to your house
i said i don't have a car because i got in a car wreck
you said you rear-ended someone and felt dumb
i said you should just buy a tank because that's a good investment
you said you drank a lot tonight but didn't get drunk

you are somewhere in florida right now

—

when you were ten you found your dad's sawed-off shotgun
we ran into the street and waved it around to scare people
when your other friends came over we hid and didn't answer the door
you were nice to me and made me food
your cousin scored negative points in laser tag and we laughed at him
your cousin died in a car crash and you told me on instant messenger one
    day but we hadn't talked for two years and i didn't know what to say so i
    pretended i wasn't there and you left your phone number and i never
    called you
but this poem isn't about how we shouldn't have laughed at your cousin for
    scoring negative points
and it isn't about how i shouldn't have ignored you on instant messenger
it isn't about me or you or your dad or your cousin
it isn't about anything

things you have emailed me
———

have you ever heard a rabbit scream, it is horrible

———

the only way to read wittgenstein is in a wooden chair with coffee. a hard wooden chair. you have to sit straight up and hate yourself the whole time. i don't know why it's important to hate yourself while reading him, but it works better when you do

but what is the definition of stupidity: 'you make stupid goals and on the way to achieving them you make stupid mistakes and in the end you're just stupid'

i woke up to no emails, the horror

thanks for the anus compliment

if i gave you a blurb it would say, 'after reading tao lin's bed i went to my room, drank, looked out the window, then broke something my dad gave me when i was five'

i think i am going to write a book about how stupid and little i am. how i do nothing. about making pizzas, holding pepperoni, in my hand, placing it on the pizza

you have to query an agent, then the agent accepts you, then the agent submits to an editor, then if the editor likes it, they submit to the publishers. what the fuck is all this shit?

i can't see lorrie moore or joy williams killing someone. if someone was killing their kids, and they got the gun, they would not shoot. they would panic. and the robber would take the gun back and they would be dead

but in your writing and talking to you. i think you would shoot the person. i think you could knife a person if you knew there were no consequences if they were annoying you bad enough. and also, i think if you were bored enough, you would rob small stores for something to do

i went to poetry.com to look at old poems i wrote like six years ago. i looked up your name. you have poems there too

the shemale looked better than half the girls i've had sex with

i want to design the perfect gun to commit suicide with. so you don't have to use your toes and it is a certain death

they find dead people all the time in abandoned buildings in youngstown. a group of people will be smoking crack, and one dies. the crackheads take the dead crackheads and leave them in an abandoned building. they don't call the police, they might send them to jail. i think it is the crack head code of honor

i used to work with retards for money, not because i care about retards. we would go bowling, and the retards would bowl 140s and get strikes. i can only bowl like 90 and get no strikes. one day one of the retards called me a retard for doing something stupid

i want to sell books in europe. at least i will not know the retardation of my readers then. and i can still be a pizza boy. and no one will know at the shop i write books and have a blog. they will treat me like i am stupid and call me a dumbass when i put green peppers on a pepperoni pizza. and i will smile, because someone thinks i'm stupid and useless. sometimes i fuck up at work and say a big word, and people stare at me and ask me how i know that, i tell them what it means, and walk away quickly

last night a cute girl in a gas station was being polite and laughing while trying to talk to me and i said, 'yeah.' and walked out of the store

we speak because we're angry, depressed, alienated, and we would probably kill ourselves, but we go on to see if we might get published. those are good common values that we share

i want to write a book where some guy is running at aliens shooting screaming, 'you dirty bastard aliens!'

i'm growing an anton chekhov facial hair pattern

in manhattan on 29th street across the avenues then over a railing there is a little beach

———

you quit school
and gave up on life
you had cancer or something so they excised your flesh
there were other problems with your lymph nodes
you came to my reading in chinatown and vomited
we had creative writing
you wrote about a dog that was a sad robot
i wrote about sad children and a giant squid
now you are an electrician
because of student loans you are fucked
there is an online game that you play
you have gained a lot of weight
you said you don't check your email anymore
i lent you money for cigarettes
'you've given up on life,' i said
you said you hadn't
i said we'd play the lottery
you said you just threw out about seventeen non-winning tickets
i said i went to atlantic city over thanksgiving and won
i said we'd go to atlantic city
you said you can't; not until you win the lottery

you took me to the beach
the beach was gray
you lay on a rock and you said it was beautiful
it was 3 a.m. and i stood there
the water was black
'let's go,' i said
'wait,' you said
i said okay
and a few minutes passed

book reviewers always praise books as 'life-affirming' because the more humans there are on earth the better

———

i click a link on the internet
i watch a video
a bullfighter in spain
pushes a sword into a bull's shoulder
the entire sword goes down into the bull
like a toothpick into a plum

and the bull keeps moving and bucking
and as it moves around
the sword cuts up its insides
and i want to see the bull's eyes
but the video is quicktime
and the size of a baby's forehead cut in half
and i turn my head
to a different angle
so that i might see the bull's eyes
but this is on a computer screen
and two-dimensional
and now the bullfighter is cutting off the bull's ears
from behind, and the bull is on the ground, and shivering
as if it were cold, and just wanted a blanket, and a bed
and i deleted this line
and i deleted this line, too, in revisions
and i deleted this line that was talking about god
and this line was also talking about god and it said something about the
universe and i deleted it
and this line kept talking about semantics and i deleted it

promise i'll vote for you

i want my TV to be two-way
and i want to throw a CD case at my TV
and have the CD case hit the president's face
and i want the president to bleed
but then smile
and wear a pink band-aid

and say that it's payback time
but say it ironically
with compassion
and forgiveness

and then throw something, a new law
at his TV, and hit me in my face
and save me, and make me unlonely
and make me change in good and irreversible ways
because that's what presidents are for
i mean, that's what presidents should be for

i mean
i don't eat animals
but i don't know politics

i mean
i just feel things
and watch TV
but i don't even watch TV

poem to end my head off

___

i haven't told you yet what i found out

that in life
when tabby dies
she dies by the laundry machine

'the other dog doesn't care,' i say repeatedly

to the side of your face on a spaceship

―――――

the day we exclude the world

'laundry machines need to stop screwing around and get real jobs;
    hamsters need larger email accounts; and i need everyone to go home

and google "under germany and outside tokyo,"'

i say later that day to the united nations

at home i think,

'the other dog can't be googled

but it has secrets'

i get out of bed

and check my email

the other dog has not emailed

the other dog is indifferent

'see,' i say to my mom, 'that dog movie lied'

'which one,' my mom says

'you think movies are real because you watch fox news,' i say to the side of
    my mom's face

and receive the nobel prize

'but really movies are processed and experienced in the mind which is
    where real life also is processed and experienced,' i say

'go on,' says the nobel prize committee

───────

'the first event (then every event) immediately necessitates an event before
    it and an event after it so if anything ever had a choice then that choice
    is spread out infinitely or else unknowably lost among all the infinite
    events which means there's no choice or there's only choice which means
    that choice is a preconception—though really any word is a
    preconception and so preconception is just another word for
    consciousness which (because everything including a planet is a
    preconception because only the nothingness which eludes
    consciousness and sits outside of everything, including itself, is not a
    preconception) is the same thing as everything and cannot be escaped
    from—which means whatever happens happens only because of being
    the cause of something else which means you didn't have a choice in
    doing, feeling, or thinking whatever you just did, felt, or thought and
    neither do i right now; but now why does it feel like i don't know and
    cannot ever know again the meanings of all these words: meaning, know,
    why, good, bad, best, exist, preconception, consciousness, sincerity, fact,
    opinion; this feels serious and frustrating because it feels beautiful but
    beautiful in a way that excludes human beings and intimidates
    consciousness from outside of consciousness by sitting there, in the
    distance, on a folding chair, thinking vague thoughts about consciousness
    and sometimes thinking that consciousness is just a very soft kind of
    pretending but mostly just thinking other things that are very vague and
    intimidating,' i say indifferently

'give back the nobel prize,' says the largest nobel prize committee

in the history of the world

and i pretend to run away

but then give it back

because the other dog doesn't care

and neither do i

———

and coffee has finally changed

it now has a tylenol cold effect
makes me blanched and lightweight
like a seashell

coffee has become tylenol cold
but tylenol cold has remained tylenol cold

and this morning
i looked in the mirror
and my face looked like tylenol cold

and no one knows why tylenol cold is two words

or if the laundry machine felt excluded when tabby died

but i don't think laundry machines even read their email

or else only read them and never respond

because i don't think laundry machines understand the concept of
    communication

i think looking at the side of your face turns life into a sad computer's dream

i think about that for a really long time

by accident

then sprint to the other dog's room

and the other dog's face is concentrating

he is writing the world's saddest email about indifference

———

and i am thinking

that maybe tomorrow i will finally decide to take caffeine pills

and snort them up my nose

one pill for each day that is not glorious

many, many, many, many, many, many

this poem has all this between each stanza:
me at work refreshing my email eight times in three seconds
my mom text-messaging me by accident, 'life is too sad without tabby'
someone on the largest dose of tylenol cold in the history of the world
    falling off a sixty-story building at night
footage on hamster news of monks fistfighting animals in the woods
    outside tokyo

remember that part
in life
when i tell you i want world war three to happen
so i can fly to germany
and save all the hamsters?

i want the world's saddest computer
to text-message me,
'do you like hamsters because they are soft?'

i want laundry machines
to drink coffee at night
and secretly collect things
that no one else will

i also want a prize
that when you squeeze it
it goes, 'congratulations; you do not believe in free will'
or, 'congratulations; your worldview is cause and effect'

———

'does it glow in the dark?' you say

and step over the world's largest hamster

and grin

the hamster is also grinning

'what if i win the dark nobel prize,' i say

to the side of your face at night

from the largest distance in the history of the world

'congratulations; you are a successful genius,' the dark nobel prize would
      say sarcastically

'many, many, many, many, many, many,' it would say mockingly

and then read the end of 'the stranger' in a high-pitched voice

that would make me laugh

and want to rob camus
with a meat cleaver
that chooses to glow in the dark

albert camus

'fucking give me all your cash,' i'd say indifferently

tonight i want to get an email from myself from the future that says, 'tao,
      there are many hamsters; tao, hamster news just said that death is really a
      form of email; and, tao, the world's saddest email about indifference is
      finally on the nobel prize committee,' and i want to meet you when we
      were in middle school; but not at school

———

but in the future in a corridor

on a spaceship going away from earth

the day we team up to win world war three

independent of the nation-states involved

and give the world to a hamster

a soft hamster

the hamster is embarrassed

'fucking give me all your cash,' i'd say to the hamster's mom

by accident

and win my second dark nobel prize; this time for 'audacity'

'camus is immature,'

it would say repeatedly

to the side of my face

'camus is just a larger hamster,'

i would think in bed

then at work

then staring at my computer
finally to the largest gathering of hamsters

in the history of the world

i would say repeatedly and in a high-pitched voice, 'albert "the sad
    hamster" camus'

at home i pretend to concentrate

on finally having the world's realest job

'i have the world's fakest job,' i pretend to think by accident

'i am always at home,' i think

and go to the store

and buy the largest laundry machine in the history of the world

only because it's on sale

'i think the largest laundry machine in the world is embarrassed at how
    often it checks its email,'

i say to the side of your face

and the side of your face is beautiful

'i think world war three might be a lot of fun,'

someone somewhere thinks

and falls off a sixty-story building

but maybe that person was right

maybe when you lose a limb an elf heals you

———

and when you die you start over outside tokyo

with an elf who has read the world's saddest email about indifference

and is now the most immature elf in the world

but

i don't know anymore

what to google

to find out what movies to see

'i don't know the meaning of the word meaning,' i say on hamster news

'i also don't know the nobel prize from tylenol cold,' i say while someone
    else is talking

'i don't know,' i say to my mom

coffee has chosen not to help me

life is too sad without tabby

elves are processed and experienced by sad computers going away from
    earth

and when i was driving tonight i felt so sad that it was frustrating

to usually indifferent monks

collecting hamsters outside tokyo

and i haven't told you yet a lot of things

———

and the best ideas are somewhere else

they took the thing that allows tylenol cold to be one word, camus to be a
    hamster, and themselves to leave; and in the world's softest-looking
    spaceship they left

and they don't need us

or we would be there now

grinning

and making choices

about what to google

what information to exclude

and who to blame

'but maybe laundry machines would finally stop screwing around and write
    the most exciting and funniest civil war poems ever,' i say a few pages
    later in the poem to end my own head off

'i am the poem to end some guy's head off,'

says the poem to end my head off

when i am least expecting it

about fifteen pages later

and sits on a folding chair in the distance

and doesn't do anything

so i take off my shoes

―――――

and go there

near it

and pretend to collect seashells

and step on a jellyfish

and go home

and stare at the computer screen

'the other dog is building a spaceship,' i think

and check tabby's email

the world's largest laundry machine has emailed

the world's saddest email

about not being able to move

it is also the world's saddest email about being put on sale

finally it is also the world's longest email

and i print it out

and while it is printing out

i google 'jellyfish poison'

without pretending that i am not thinking about the side of your face

i see million dollar baby, starring clint eastwood, with my mom

_____

i say, 'why are they playing evil music for the boxer who isn't hilary swank'

my mom says, 'clint eastwood is in great shape, look at him, he's more than ten years older than your dad'

in the parking lot i say, 'why was the young black boxer so evil; i hate that'

my mom says, 'clint eastwood had two needles, remember; i bet one was for himself,' and she laughs a little and she looks at me and i look at her and then i laugh a little too

on the way home i am driving and i make this very wide turn through this massive intersection; and i am driving very fast and i am a little out of control and while i am making this insane turn, sideswiping across three or four lanes, i look at my mom and i grin at her really big and her face looks a little blank and i feel really happy and really sad at the same time

the next night i am eating pineapple chunks when my mom appears suddenly beside me with her living will

she has the pages of her living will folded back and she points at where it says that she does not want to be put on a respirator or feeding tube or whatever artificial life thing if it ever comes to that

she points out the exact sentence where it says all that and she tells me to look and i look and i see that it has her signature there and she pats my back and runs away and goes to sleep because she is in her pajamas and it is very late

i finish eating my pineapple chunks and then i drink a glass of orange juice, and then i eat two bananas, a huge thing of grapes, a small container of blueberries, an apple, a banana, and a gigantic bowl of noodles with vegetables in it

you are my mom

——

you cried in your bedroom when your sister's husband died of the flu
    you came out of your bedroom and told me that your sister's husband
    died of the flu and you grinned
and i ran away
and i ran away upstairs into my room and played the drums and used a lot
    of cymbals and my ears rang

when i think of grapefruits my heart beats faster

―――――

when i can't sleep i see fruit at night
and i know i must eat it so fast that it's like a cobra striking a teenager's face
but the fruit is big and i know i have to chew it first
but i also know i must consume it immediately
so fast that only a stop-motion camera can capture my movements on film
    when i devour a watermelon

my heart beats faster because it's impossible to feed myself fruit that
    quickly and this gives me anxiety and fear

but maybe it's not impossible
because one night i ate twelve tangerines
and when i looked at my bowl of tangerine peels it was obvious i had just
    inhaled a dozen tangerines in less than a microsecond; and i carried the
    bowl to my brother and said, 'feel how heavy,' and he did

and the next afternoon my brother came in the apartment at 2 p.m. and i
    was asleep
and he said, 'i haven't pooped in four days'
and i thought i was dreaming
but it was in real life because later i told my mom and my mom was not
     shocked

my mom said, 'your brother has always had a problem with pooping;
    how about you?'
i said, 'what do you mean "how about you?"'
she said, 'do you have a problem with pooping?'
and i wasn't shocked or afraid because it's normal for my mom to be
    concerned about my health and for the rest of my life i wasn't nervous,
    shocked, surprised, or afraid about anything except for this one day in
    december when i felt all those things at once and couldn't believe i was
    actually alive and cried myself to sleep

i am 'you' to you

———

i believe that coffee can solve many of my problems

i do not really exist because i live vicariously through myself because i
    experience my own life through you through me and also because my
    experience of art is through what i imagine your experience of art is and
    art is life vicarious and life is void vicarious

i am lost from that last sentence

i got lost

the rest of this poem will not make sense

the rest of my life

yeah

wait

buddhism says the identity is not even real

you say your spleen fell in your lung

i say don't you don't need a spleen

i drive one hundred and twenty miles per hour and take a digital
    photograph of my speedometer

Washington Mutual is A Bank That is Everywhere

―――

I had an urge one hour ago. To write poems
that make no sense, and
I felt happy. Stabbed
by hooded black youth.
Shocked by the willingness of grade-schoolers
to kill me. And eat my heart. The things that do not happen to me
each day. I feel
like shit. My life
is good, fantastic. I am not deformed. Thank you.

There should be something about you
in this poem. But

there is just me, being stupid.
Putting shampoo on things. My roommate's shampoo. Uncouth. My heart
is a bar of soap. White, flashing. Soap
is clean. Admit it. That it will kill you
if you eat it
probably. I mean, look
at this poem. Where are you. I love life. November. Wonderful. The sun.
     A cloud
just said something. I don't know what it said.
I wasn't paying attention. I don't care.

i Will Like The Things i Dislike, Hate, Or Am indifferent Towards

My head is a car. I drive
a different car. People laugh at me
from skyscrapers. I buy one-thousand-
page-novels. It hurts to move. I stare at things
that are close to me physically. My brain
was at Wal-Mart. It was on sale. It wasn't
fair. The weekend is lonely. For lunch
I have dinner. Instead of feeling sad, I transform
into a nerd. It is just a matter
of semantics. Don't ever
do what you are doing right now
again, I tell myself, each moment, thinking.

April

____

I stood outside St. Mark's bookstore and you wore a colorful shirt. I wanted to hold your hand. We went to the movie. I couldn't talk and maybe I refused to talk and you said, 'Stop being an asshole.' I was shy and you made me hate myself.

The movie had a message. It told me to enjoy my life while I was alive. 'I know,' I said to the movie.

It was raining outside and you walked faster than me and I wanted to sit down. We stopped to say goodbye. 'Come with me to the grocery store,' I said. You said okay and you seemed happy and we went and I was happy.

In the grocery store you stared at me from a distance. 'What are you doing?' I said. I wanted to play. 'I have homework,' you said from a distance. I bought a banana.

I told you I didn't want to walk home. I ate my banana and I said it was disgusting and I said, 'I hate bananas,' and I complained a little about life and you left and I walked home.

walking home in cold weather

---

i give money to a homeless man
there is another homeless man
i give him money
there are two homeless people and i give them money
the street has snow
i cannot play; or build an igloo
there are enough homeless men to have a snowfight
i am not charismatic enough to organize a snowfight
it is january
it is raining not snowing
i am not a little boy afraid of sharks when gurgling salt water
i am detached from whatever i am about to think
inside my room i walk to my bed
i should have cartwheeled to it
i dream that people who get speeding tickets are irresponsible
i am detaching the cop's arm from his body
he was punching me in the face
i will kill anyone who hurts my emotions
'i will kill you!' i scream at a scared little boy
i will monitor his email for the rest of his life

my brother is vacationing on a mountain with his girlfriend and i found out from my dad
___

i am happy
it is 1:07 a.m. and i am very happy
i just ate six nests of angel hair pasta
i have garlic, pepper, olive oil, tomato sauce
they sit here next to me like little people
tinier people that i will eat that sit next to me like friends
i sit on an air mattress because i am living with my brother
my brother is a graphic designer who has a studio apartment
i am listening to a mixed CD
the mixed CD says, 'taking all i know about nihilism
and trying to build it into a life'
and i am very happy
i am not hiding away a lot of sadness
i am not
i am happy
you can't stop me
i won't die
my happiness will glow and my glow will kill death
so happy

———

very happy
not to be interpreted as having only a happy facade
i am not to be interpreted as being delusional or stupid or on drugs
i am aware of death, loneliness, that time only goes in one direction;
    still i am happy
i am not on drugs
i am really happy and this is the truth
do you believe me
you don't believe me
but i am
it is 1:10 a.m. and i am alone in my brother's studio apartment and i just
    grinned
(it is 2:24 a.m. inside of this parenthetical and i am doing revisions on this
    poem and i am not that happy anymore but thirsty; but not thirsty
    enough to go drink something)
i sit on an air mattress and i am happier than you are
you are serious and i am happy
you can go away and go home because i am happy
you aren't here but you can still go home because i am kicking you out of
    my room
get off my air mattress because i am kicking you out of my brother's studio
    apartment
i kick you in the knees
one time for no reason you kicked the back of my knee like it was a real
    maneuver that you had practiced and learned
a maneuver for making me crumple and fall
i was impressed
you have impressed me
thank you
i like you
i am happy
i lick your tongue
i stare at you
i order a snowball from alaska and throw it at you in august when you are
    not looking and i miss and the snowball goes behind a school bus and no
    one knows; no one knows where babies come from

February

At the bank I felt like I was in Super Mario World. I pointed at things that made me feel that way and I pointed at the ceiling and we went to a furniture store. We sat there. And we went to a bookstore.

You said you wanted to read 'Against Love.' I said Lorrie Moore had a character with a like-life instead of a love-life and you said that was good. 'Lorrie Moore is good,' I said.

A little girl ran by with about fifteen books and you said she was a genius.

We read a children's book that told children to eat hot dogs. And we hid it. And you pointed at Infinite Jest. I said my girlfriend read it and you got quiet. You were quiet and asked why I didn't live with my girlfriend. 'I don't have a girlfriend,' I said. 'You just said you did,' you said. I said I meant ex-girlfriend and a Barnes and Noble person stood above us.

The Barnes and Noble lady wore a kimono. She freaked out and gave a lecture about where to sit and we paid attention and she ran away. I looked at your face. I said something and you laughed.

You snorted when you laughed and I said that you snorted. You were louder and happier than before. I slapped you a little. I said I was wearing kimonos to work from now on. I brought you the punk planet with my story in it.

'Is it real?' you said. 'You said everything you write is real.'

I said I didn't know and I said maybe. 'Just read it,' I said. 'Just read it later,' I said.

You read it and I looked at the side of your face. The story had my ex-girlfriend and a guitar and you asked me if I played guitar. I said, 'I don't know.' I said I played drums. You said you were twenty-six and made minimum wage at Barnes and Noble and wore kimonos to work. And we used escalators to get to the first floor.

And we made it. I said I was going to pants you. And when we got outside it was nighttime.

At That Leftover Crack Concert Two Years Before i Met You

I think it would be fun if I were the saddest thing in the world.

I think people would band together to make me an award. At the ceremony it would be very touching. They would carry me and I would crowd-surf them even if I were something that doesn't move like a shoe or an ant that died. Because I think the saddest thing in the world might be a dead ant. They work so hard and I think most of them die from exhaustion. They never sleep or eat or drink water. I told you one time that I wanted a tattoo on my arm of ants underwater and a squid. You said that ants underwater must be the saddest thing in the world. You ignored the squid, but I didn't disagree about that other thing you said. It was on the Internet where this happened and not in real life and I think I just stared at the screen and felt a little sad, but mostly just excited and happy.

I wonder, would I be happy in a fascist society? Because fascism doesn't let you complain about the government then I guess it encourages you to complain about interpersonal issues, personal issues, and other non-governmental things like the weather and death.

Like, why does there have to be death? I always complain about how bad I feel and lonely. I don't think a fascist would shoot me with a rifle for complaining in one-page poems about feeling depressed and unloved because that just takes the blame away from the government and gives it to me in the form of a Microsoft Word document. Fascist societies are strange but I think they can be fun. I don't believe I would make a good dictator because if I stood on a balcony people would want me to give them an unambiguous, ruthless, and deadly speech. But I would probably just want to jump off the balcony if it wasn't too high so that I could crowd-surf my thousands or millions of people.

I think I would panic and drive into a building if I was in Manhattan and a fire truck had its sirens on. In Florida when I'm driving I always use ambulances as an excuse to make illegal U-turns and to drive over medians and do other fun and provocative things with my car. One time an ambulance was coming and I made a U-turn and saw a tree and calmly drove there and knocked it down then saw a shrub and went to that and ran it over like a lawn mower. I felt patriotic because I was trying harder than everyone else to get out of the way of the ambulance.

    Just kidding. I would never knock down a tree because I am afraid the car might explode, like they do in movies. I know that movies are fake but sometimes it feels like I am inside of them. I'm a bad actor in real life and always out-of-character but in a movie that would make me a good actor because I would seem authentically bad at social situations. One time that I didn't think at all that I was inside of a movie was when I was at a Leftover Crack concert in Brooklyn. The guitarist was pissed because there were four eight-year-olds on stage and they kept running off and stage-diving and it was obvious they weren't listening to the music at all. The guitarist had songs about shooting heroin in alleyways and the joys of poverty. He grew up in India. I felt really bad for him because he couldn't enjoy himself because of eight-year-olds. I thought, if he can't enjoy himself because of four small children, then he must feel depressed and agitated all the time in his normal life, right? I asked myself because I wasn't sure. But really I was. I knew it was true. He would always be a sad and grumpy man.

    But I still felt uncertain, as if someone were lying to me all the time no matter what and it was impossible to ever feel like the most okay thing in the world.

2006/2007 Action Books Titles

---

you are a little bit happier than i am by Tao Lin
Winner of the 2005 December Prize
ISBN: 0-9765692-3-X
ISBN: 978-0-9765692-3-7

Telescope by Sandy Florian
ISBN: 0-9765692-4-8
ISBN: 978-0-9765692-4-4

You go the words by Gunnar Björling,
translated by Frederik Hertzberg
Scandinavian Series #2
ISBN: 0-9765692-5-6
ISBN:: 978-0-9765692-5-1

The Edge of Europe by Pentti Saarikoski,
translated by Anselm Hollo
Scandinavian Series #3
ISBN: 0-9765692-6-4
ISBN: 978-0-9765692-6-8

lobo de labio by Laura Solórzano
translated by Jen Hofer
ISBN: 0-9765692-7-2
ISBN: 978-0-9765692-7-5

2005 Action Books Titles

———

The Hounds of No by Lara Glenum
ISBN:0-97656592-1-3

My Kafka Century by Arielle Greenberg
ISBN:0-97656592-2-1

Remainland: Selected Poems of Aase Berg,
translated by Johannes Göransson
Scandinavian Series #1
ISBN:0-97656592-0-5